Praise for
A Story and a Point

I have known Andy for eight years. He is the real deal; honest, vulnerable, deep and funny to boot! In this book, you will find him plain spoken, with down-to-earth practical insight on everyday life with a good dose of humor. He puts the cookies on the lower shelve so that we can all reach them and learn from his experiences.

Andy's great story-telling skills will grab and hold your attention. Some writing and teaching that I have partaken of tends (at times) to be too heavy and laborious. Not with Andy who wonderfully approaches life with a light touch and solid humor. His writing style reminds me of author and business consultant Patrick, Lencioni who tells a story and then squeezes the valuable lesson out of the story just told.

Even Andy's chapter titles will elicit a laugh; maybe not a deep belly laugh, but at least a quiet chuckle...guaranteed! Each chapter has a story and a point; yes, he does have a point. They're not just stories to entertain and tickle your funny bone a bit, but rather to get you thinking about some very important issues in life and leadership.

I'm not sure we will ever see Andy on SNL, but I would nominate him for at least one appearance. If Andy was ever looking for a 2nd career (not that he wants or needs one) he could be a stand-up comedian; but a comedian with a *"Point."*

As you dive into the book, have your pen or high-lighter in hand as there will be things you'll want to note and remember for future reference and personal application.

Dave Kraft
Author of "Leaders Who Last"
Leadership coach, consultant, and seminar presenter

A Story and A Point

Find Meaning in Everyday Life

By Andy Kerr

& Paul Macosko

DEDICATION

One of my favorite John Maxwell sayings is, "*If you see a turtle on a fence post, you know it had help getting there.*" So many people have encouraged, supported and mentored me throughout my life and I am extremely grateful for each one. I would not be who I am today if not for your positive impact.

I would first and foremost like to thank my wife, Jennifer Kerr. Jen, you have been a co-adventurer with me and often the lead explorer. You have dreamed with me, challenged me to go beyond what I thought I was capable of doing, and partnered with me to tell a much better story of our lives. This project is from beginning to end, a result of your encouragement. I am truly grateful for your strength, your ability to see reality and to speak the truth in love. I am constantly in awe of your ability to do so many things well; not least of which is an uncanny ability to take a good thing and make it great. That is exactly what you have done with my life— taken my good life and made it great. I love you Jenny.

To my dad Matt Kerr, the master storyteller, from whom I've learned the art of telling stories: You trained us boys as your apprentices with new jokes and great stories. You really are the original "Story and a Point" guy, constantly dispensing wisdom through anecdotes, humorous one-liners, wise sayings and riveting tales. You weren't just there with a great story, you were there in my corner cheering me on for every game, every meet, every accomplishment and very literally for the charity boxing event. Thank you so much for helping me tell a better story with my words and my life.

To my mom Diane Ward: You were the story. You have spent your life quietly serving and helping everyone around you. You gave your love away, demonstrating to us boys how to love and care for others. As a child, you went with your aunt to help at the Erie City Mission. You returned as a volunteer later in life and now I get to carry on your legacy as the Chaplain of the Erie City Mission. You were always an adventurer—ready at any moment to jump in the car and go somewhere new. You taught me the art of living a great story in order to tell one. Because of you, I try to love everyone I meet and make every day an adventure. Thank you so much.

To my two brothers, Bryan and Jason: You are both amazing men and great fathers. Some of the best stories are the ones we share—many of which I promise not to tell Mom or Dad about. Both of you are geniuses in the areas of your passions and you inspire me to be better at what I do and to have fun doing it.

Jay, I love how you see the world. Your creative perspective has helped me see the world through new eyes. Your passion for life and adventure challenges me to think more creatively and pursue what I love more deeply. Thank you.

Bryan, you are the intersection of technical skill and compassion for people. You have always used your powers to fix things for good. You rescue people from being stranded, stuck and broken down; helping to get them back on track with where they want to go. Whether it is literally or figuratively, your kindness has rescued so many people—including me. I am incredibility grateful for you.

To my personal coach and friend, Dave Kraft: You have been instrumental in guiding me as a coach in my life, in ministry and now in my business. Your book "Leaders Who Last" was transformative in my life. It was a catalyst in the decision to hire a life coach—not knowing you were one of the coaches at the place I called. You have been a tremendous example of a Godly man. Now almost 80 years old, you continue to live with vigor and vitality, impacting leaders and encouraging them to finish well. Being a successful writer and published author, I am humbled and honored you agreed to write the forward to this book.

To my niece, Rebecca Kerr: At a very young age you told me that I needed to write a book. We have discussed and brainstormed many ideas. You may not know just how important of a role you have played in this book becoming a reality. I can't wait to read your book someday. I know you have one in you; just don't wait until you are old like me to write it. Thank you for believing in me.

To my friend, Paul Macosko: I can't tell you how much it means to me to partner with you on this project. So many of these stories are ones we have shared. You have an amazing ability to combine humor and deep insight—whether writing or speaking. Your heart is gold and your integrity unsurpassed. You put the "grit" in integrity. You have always inspired me to go deeper in my faith, to have more fun no matter the task, and to serve others along the way. Faith, fun, and service are like breathing for you and you are changing this world for the good just by being yourself. Thank you, my friend.

To my friend, Erin Layden: You are brilliant. You are also very kind and helpful whenever I have found myself stuck. You have been so gracious through this entire process. I cannot thank you enough for guiding this project and making it excellent. You jumped in and gave this book legs. It is hard to find someone with your level of expertise and it wouldn't have happened without you. Thank you for helping me tell my story.

To my friend, Rachel Lusky: You have incredible design skills. Thank you for being patient in this process of writing my first book. I hope we can collaborate on many more projects like this.

-Andy Kerr

I am deeply grateful to Andy Kerr for allowing me a chance to see and describe the profoundly meaningful life that lies before us all. Andy's ability to turn the ordinary into the extraordinary has been a joy to capture into words and stories. Also, I am so very thankful to my wife Harilyn and to my two boys, Riley and Beckett, who constantly push me out of my comfort zone — while encouraging me to pursue the gifts God has placed inside of me. They have blessed me beyond measure. With gratitude I thank them for the freedom and space they give me to create, even through difficult times and seasons. Finally, I thank the many others who have worked to help bring this book to life. Erin Layden is a literary titan and superb encourager, Rachel Lusky is a creative genius, and Jennifer Kerr is a behind-the-scenes hero through each chapter — as well as a true co-adventurer with Andy. For them and for God's grace, which accomplishes infinitely more than we could ever ask or imagine, I express my most sincere thanks.

- Paul Macosko

Table of Contents

"Shirt Unbuttoned, a Mirror and Self Reflection"

What's the Story?

Far too often there is a strange gap between perception and reality. Some summers ago, while serving as a small-town college pastor, I decided to throw a party for some of the students I was serving. Knowing food to be the great attractor of college students, I set out with a good friend to gather the snacks we needed to make our party a hit.

Small towns are funny, aren't they? There aren't many places you can go without being recognized; and you surely can't get out of a store without a handful of unexpected conversations.

As we weaved our way through the store picking up our party food, we had a few of these unexpected conversations with students we knew. Even in the checkout line, we found ourselves standing right next to a girl we recognized from our campus ministry. Small towns—right? Making small talk, I asked about her major and how school was going as we talked about our ministry and the upcoming party. After making our way through the checkout line, my friend and I were celebrating another successful small-town shopping trip and another set of positive connections made with students.

It wasn't until we were standing in front of the large glass doors that marked the threshold between building and parking lot that I noticed something about myself—something that left a strange gap between the perception I had of myself and a portrait of reality. The shirt I was wearing was completely unbuttoned, and it was a Hawaiian shirt at that! What was I thinking?

Recounting our trip, I thought about how I was coming across to those I had seen in the store. Reality in my head painted me as an inquisitive college pastor. Yet, reality in the mirror made me look like a creepy old guy. There was a strange gap between the perception I held of myself and reality. It didn't help that my good friend soothed my perceptive distortions with, "I thought that was the look you were going for!"

Here's the Point.

So often, we fail to see reality as it is. The gap between what we think is happening and what is actually happening often goes unnoticed. How detrimental this gap is. As psychology reminds us, reality is always our friend. This gap is bridged by a set of mirrors positioned to accurately reflect reality back onto us. But what do these mirrors look like, and how can we use them to see reality?

Let's talk about that for a second: the first mirror I reflect in —or rather reflect on—are books. Often while reading about great companies, entrepreneurs or world changers, I see with clarity the values and ideals I need to embrace; as well as what inside of me needs to change or adapt. Books help me to see where I am at, and where I need to go with clarity. What are you reading? What are your learning? How can you be a lifetime learner and use the mirror of literature to see and shape your reality?

The second mirror is personal reflection. In twelve-step addiction recovery programs, this is more commonly called Step Ten. Taking intentional time in the morning or evening to reflect on the day can help paint a clear picture of your life's realities. Asking questions like: What did I accomplish today? Did I achieve all the goals set for the day? Where did I succeed and where did I drop the ball today? These questions can shed new light on reality.

Finally, there is the mirror of having an inner circle. Those you know and trust deeply are great candidates for a strong inner circle. Hand-picking people who carry the weight of friendship with an iron sharpening iron strength—while ruthlessly working to eliminate the mediocrity of mere acquaintance—is no small task, and not everyone is up for the job.

Each of us should strive to have a strong inner circle of truth tellers no matter the flaw, no matter the time. A strong inner circle has great power to reveal the truth about our strengths, weaknesses and those things we need to change. These people can help identify our blind spots and push us to be the best we can be.

Do you have some or all of these mirrors set up in your life? If not, what can you do today to put these mirrors in place? Let's bridge the strange gap that can exist between our perceptions and reality.

Reflection and Discussion Questions

1. What mirrors are you using to shape your reality?
2. What steps can you take today to set up positive mirrors in your life?

Watch the accompanying video "Shirt Unbuttoned, a Mirror and Self-reflection" at https://www.youtube.com/watch?v=ICa4dzbFna0&t=4s

Notes

_____

_____

_____

_____

_____

_____

_____

_____

_____

_____

_____

_____

_____

_____

_____

_____

_____

_____

_____

_____

_____

_____

2

"The Lobster Lady of Maine"

What's the Story?

What's the worst job you've ever had? Maybe a question like this requires a deep reach into distant memories. Or maybe the answer is as near as your drive home from work today. Either way, to answer the question, what makes up the worst job ever, I imagine, is different for each of us. Sometimes the answer is obvious, and sometimes we're more oblivious—as the story of the Lobster Lady of Maine goes.

Let me explain.

A few years back, my wife Jen and I decided to travel to the coast of Maine as a vacation destination. The way we vacation is to take a map, throw it out, and get off the beaten path to discover what's really out there. We enjoy making up the journey as it's happening, with a few pointers from those who have gone before. "Of course, you need to try the lobster" seemed to be the common consensus of those we know who had been to Maine. Those especially lobster-savvy even added, "And make sure it's cold water lobster from a shack, not a restaurant." If you've been to Maine, then you know what I'm talking about. This sounded like a delicious adventure to my wife and I, so we accepted the tip, packed up the car and headed out.

After driving up the East coast and reaching Maine, we found a lobster shack. We headed inside, sat down and a very sweet lady came out from the back of the restaurant to take our order. "What would you like to eat?" she politely said. "We would like two lobsters," we eagerly replied. She wrote down our order and disappeared into the kitchen.

After a few minutes, she returned to our table with giant salt water tears streaming down her face. I was quite surprised by her sadness. "Ma'am, is there something wrong?" I asked. "Well," she began. "When I put the lobsters in the pot, I get really sad. It just makes me want to cry every time I put a lobster in and then I get mad at myself." Without a tone of trying-not-to-state-the-obvious, I replied, "Ma'am, you are probably in the wrong line of work because I'm sure you do this on a very regular basis."

Was the lobster lady in the wrong profession?   The conclusion I netted was a cold-water-yes.

Here's the Point.

Sometimes we take some wrong turns on the path to self-discovery. We get off the beaten path, start walking down a road that looks like a step toward our calling, and find our self in a place where we just don't fit. Worse yet, we mistake this wrong turn as a destination and we stop moving toward our calling. It is there that we find ourselves immersed into rhythms and patterns of consistent life; blinding us to the obvious dysfunction we're choosing to function in. In other terms, we become stuck. And once we're stuck, it's difficult to get out. Have you been there before? Maybe you're there now.

Maybe you have a job that makes you cry. Maybe there is a situation in your life you know needs to change. Maybe you have a problem with motivation. What kind of change do you need to make and why are you waiting to make the change?

So often we choose to put off changing, when changing can actually make our lives better. We have to be willing to go through a temporary inconvenience for a permanent improvement.

If this thought strikes a chord with you, maybe you are stuck. Maybe today needs to be the day in which you get back onto the road; acknowledging that you haven't reached your destination yet. You're still on a journey and the road before you is taking you to a greater place. Who can you seek out to help you thorough the changes you need to make? Who can keep you accountable toward moving toward improvement? Lasting change comes from accountable community.

"Life is too short not to do something that matters." (Seth Godin, Linchpin: Are You Indispensable?, Penguin Group 2011.) Even the smallest step toward something that matters is worth it. Will you take that step today?

Reflection and Discussion Questions

1. In what areas of your life are you feeling stuck?
2. What is holding you back from making the change(s) you need?
3. Are there people in your life that can help you on the journey through change? Who are they? Will they hold you accountable?

Watch the accompanying video "Lobster Lady" at https://www.youtube.com/watch?v=7ZFLS2aJalE&t=1s

Notes

3

"Opossums and Coping"

What's the Story?

If an opossum had a mission statement, it would probably be this: "I'm going to eat well or die trying." The evidence is all over the road confirming this assumption. Here's how I came to believe in this marsupial mission statement of sorts.

While driving across a typical road in Northwest Pennsylvania, I noticed him, and he noticed my Ford Ranger. This particular opossum, in full view of my truck and hungry for breakfast, thoughtfully stopped in his tracks to consider his options—both lying just steps in front of him. I'm guessing he weighed the pros and cons, considered the marsupial mission statement given to him by his forefathers, and then made his decision.

He decided to go for it, running into the road right in front of the Ranger. The ball was now in my court forcing me to consider my options. At that moment, I became super grateful for the increased suspension in my truck as well as my catlike reflexes. Both worked together as I swerved around the opossum, while steadily maintaining four wheels on the road—win.

This moment left me asking one big question; namely, "Why do opossums seemingly want to die?" I couldn't figure it out. I polled google as I pondered at the next red light. Here's what I discovered: 8.3 million opossums are killed on the roadways of the United States annually because one, they eat roadkill and two, they are slow. Opossums have developed a crazy coping mechanism for survival in which they go to roadways to eat roadkill as an easy source of food.

What the opossum forefathers failed to take into account when developing their mission statement was that if you're slow, and hang out on the road eating food, you're probably going to get killed. This coping mechanism for survival was literally killing them.

Here's the Point.

Each of us develop coping mechanisms to survive. We adapt to our environments; we seek ways to make life easier; and sometimes these coping mechanisms we develop—that initially seem helpful—become destructive in our lives.

Tension, stress and shame often lead us to do things outside of our values. The stress of survival pushes us to act in a way that actually becomes harmful for us to live. Coping mechanisms like over-working; over-indulging; under-resting; pushing others down in the path toward success; living inauthentically with our feelings and emotions become our choice methods of survival. All of these are adaptive behaviors that can keep us stuck and unable to grow into our full potential. What coping mechanisms do you use? Are they hurting you? Are they becoming destructive in your life? Maybe they are even killing you.

Take some time to identify your coping mechanisms. Write them down. There is power when we acknowledge reality and write down our findings. That's the first step to changing.

Once coping mechanisms are identified, who can you talk to about them? Maybe a counselor, a mentor, or a life coach? You can change today. You can get help. You can begin to step away from these things and step into a new, more healthy way of life that utilizes your strengths, gifts and potential.

An opossum constantly lives just shy of becoming a statistic. The coping mechanisms we develop can leave us living just shy of becoming a statistic as well. We can live under a different paradigm. The mission statement we adhere to should be one that we live by—and not what we die by.

Reflection and Discussion Questions

1. Take some time to identify some of your coping mechanisms. What are they?

2. Are your coping mechanisms hurting you, or helping you?

Watch the accompanying video "Opossums and Coping" at https://www.youtube.com/watch?v=ioFPO-aWVmw

Notes

4

"Goo Gone"

What's the Story?

What is this stuff?" I thought to myself while frantically staring at a spot I discovered on my suit. I had just gotten dressed for a Sunday morning speaking engagement when I noticed the goo-like drop on the front of my suit. Those who know me would say that I'm never early, sometimes on time and often running late to events. At this point, I was in the third category, which combined with the goo sighting prompted a mini-freak-out moment.

In this panicked state, while considering a list of options, it hit me that I saw a bottle of Goo Gone just the other day. I had goo on my suit and there was a substance called Goo Gone—I

19

knew right where it was. This was surely what I was looking for. Success was inevitable.

Sure enough, after applying the Goo Gone, I was "goo" free. The Goo Gone took the goo right off and for about ten seconds I was in the clear. About eleven seconds later, what left me "goo" free, also left me looking "goo"-fy. You see, the Goo Gone took the goo off, but in its place was a larger and more noticeable stain on my suit—yikes.

Had I read the bottle; or "goo"gled cautions for using the substance; or even talked to my wife (in the very next room) I would have found encouragement to heed an alternate course of action. Now, what was potentially unnoticeable became a true bright spot on my suit, in my conversations that day, and in this chapter.

Here's the Point.

Rarely are our first reactions the best reactions. Emotions often cloud judgement, irrationality takes over, and rather than exercising clear problem solving skills, we recoil with knee-jerk reactions and watch small dilemmas devolve into disasters. Our gut-level, visceral attempts at quick fixes often makes things much worse.

How do we stop the insanity? Let me propose two solutions under one common umbrella. First, the umbrella of Proverbs which says, "Plans go wrong for lack of advice; many advisers bring success." (Proverbs 15:22) Under this umbrella we see the two solutions; advice and advisers.

Let's focus on advice for a second. Do we ask for advice when we're in a dilemma, or would we rather go it alone? Do we try to handle life with our own wisdom; using our own solutions driven by our own reactions? I confess—I'm guilty. The proof is in the "goo" spot. Can you imagine how different life would look if we trained ourselves not to honor first reactions as solutions, but to seek advice when confronted with a challenge. We'd be a lot more humble, and a lot more successful at life navigation. Where do you need to stop and ask for help?

That begs the second solution because in order to ask for help, we need someone to ask for help—we need advisers.

To quote another proverb, one of African origin, "If you want to go quickly, go alone. If you want to go far, go together." We need community to navigate life. We are not islands; we are more like communities on continents. We are created to need one another and stick together.

Who is in your problem solving community? Who are your advisers? Who can you trust with your challenges to offer quality advice? Did you know that having the right people around you can help turn our issues into improvements and our predicaments into progress? These same people can even help turn good ideas into great ideas—true assets in our life catalyzing positive growth and success.

We need to ask for advice, and need the help of advisers to see success.

Learn from this "goo"ru. Let's not react to situations; let's look for good people to surround ourselves with and let's see our spots become the spotlight that shows us where we need to grow.

Reflection and Discussion Questions

1. Do you seek advice when you are in a difficult situation? Or do you try and work through it on your own?

2. What areas of your life, or difficult situations could use some advisers?

3. Do you have a community of people who you trust to give you advice on your challenges?

4. What steps can you take today, to start seeking sound advice and move towards success?

Watch the accompanying video "Goo Gone" at https://www.youtube.com/watch?v=TTzWDQY3Ja8&t=1s

Notes

5

"Bar and Grill"

What's the Story?

In some households, Sunday night means football. In our house, Sunday night means take-out. Our Sunday night take-out tradition truly is one of our favorites, because neither my wife, nor I enjoy cooking. We live in a wonderful age where seven digits punched into a phone will connect you with a person ready to prepare whatever your appetite is craving. A half hour later, with no dishes to be done, you're enjoying lunch, dinner, a snack, or just a typical mid-evening pizza fix.

One particular Sunday night, I called in our order, and soon drove to the bar & grill to pick it up. Upon walking in, I immediately noticed how unusually packed the place was. I had to weave my way through the crowd in search of a bartender to grab my take-out order. Around the bar, there was only one open spot to sneak in—right in front of a huge pitcher of beer next to a half empty glass. At this point, I was a hungry opportunist and this was my opportunity, so I snuck in. Seconds later, I got the bartender's attention, alerted her to my take-out order and payed for the food. She indicated that the food was almost ready and made her way back into the kitchen to check on its status.

Have you ever had a moment that seemed to happen in slow motion? I was about to have one. All of a sudden, an arm moving at a snail's pace reached down across my shoulder towards the beer pitcher. In perfect harmony, my head turned to see who owned this arm, and subsequently whose spot I may have been occupying around the bar.

I quickly apologized to the arm, and hoped that the gentleman it was attached to would also hear it. Gratefully, the gentleman was quick and polite to respond with, "Dude, don't worry about it. It's cool. Just relax, it's all good." "Thanks man," I said, "I am actually just getting take-out and heading home." Our conversation continued with him saying, "No man, this is your time. Tonight is your time. I just want you to have the time of your life." "Well, thanks, I appreciate that. I'm going to do my best." I responded.

There were two things I gathered from our brief conversation: I was definitely in this gentleman's spot at the bar, and this gentleman had a few beers prior to my arrival. Gratefully the bartender returned with my food and after grabbing it and a bro-hug from my new friend, I headed back out toward home to enjoy take-out night.

Here's the Point.

I was driving home that night, thinking about how strange this occurrence was, when the point hit me. This gentleman, potentially under the influence, left an influence on me when he said, "I want you to have the time of your life." What is having the time of your life? Well, here's my thoughts:

I was picking up food from a place I really enjoyed. I had money in my pocket to buy the food that someone else made for me. I was in a vehicle that I owned, driving home to hang out with my wife (my favorite person), to eat dinner together in a house that we own, in a city that we love and it all hit me, this is the time of my life.

In that moment, I was challenged to think about how many times I let moments get by without realizing how special they are. I'll challenge you to the same question—how many time of your life moments pass before you without notice? So often we're in a holding pattern, waiting for the next thing: the weekend, the next job, a new relationship, or for the drama to cease. We fail to miss the time of your life moments we're actually living in.

Life is a series of time of your life moments that are happening all around. As we live in a pattern of waiting, we often miss the blessing of the present life that is happening around us. Sad to say, we can even wait our life away.

We need to take the opportunities in front of us today, in our present reality, to live with gratitude for what we have and to make the best out of each moment. Through living in the present moment at the bar and grill—on a random Sunday take out night—I was reminded about how precious each moment is. We can learn from anyone if we'll be humble enough to let them teach us.

My hope and prayer is that you don't wait for life to happen but you take the opportunity to see the time of your life moments right in front of you. I hope you take the moments of today to be grateful for everything God has given you and has allowed you to have. Sometimes the best of life is experienced as we live fully embracing what's right before us.

The present is truly a gift; open it; embrace it; live in it—it's yours. I hope you have the time of your life.

Reflection and Discussion Questions

1. What does having the time of your life look like to you?
2. Do you allow moments to pass by without stopping to acknowledge how special they are?
3. What opportunities are you allowing to pass by in your present reality because your focus is on the future?

Watch the accompanying video "Bar and Grill" at https:// www.youtube.com/watch?v=TEyoWJws6zA

Notes

6

"Shuffling"

What's the Story?

It's been said that boys are like puppies; they need to go outside often. This was definitely true for me and my two brothers. We grew up in a small, snowbelt town in rural Pennsylvania close to Lake Erie. Those familiar with this area know that winters in the Great Lakes region seem to last from October to April. During this span of months, you have a better chance of seeing lake effect snow than the sun. Because of this, winter posed a serious set of challenges for my two brothers and I (and probably more so for my parents) as we were always looking for fun things to do outside.

Our two favorite winter activities were sled riding and ice skating. If it had an incline, we rode sleds down it. If it was frozen over, we ice-skated on top of it.

We frequently trudged out with shovels and ice skates to find ponds and watering holes to skate on top of. Upon arrival at one of our makeshift ice rinks, we shoveled away the top layers of snow to reveal the rough and bumpy ice coating underneath. After that, we'd skate, play hockey, or invent a game as we had fun expending our storehouses of winter energy. I learned to skate at a very young age.

At age 6, my parents took me to a local ice skating rink and I noticed how smooth, and flat the ice was. You could skate and skate for hours—it was awesome. Soon after, I can remember them enrolling me in a beginner's class to learn how to ice skate better.

Now, this was a class of beginners and I had a great advantage over them, because I had already been skating for a couple of years now. Some of the kids laced up two-bladed ice skates and prepared for their first time out on the ice. Meanwhile, I laced up my one-bladed skates and glided out onto the ice.

Once everyone was out on the ice, the teacher placed a brightly colored cone a few yards in front of us and asked that we do our best to skate out around it and back. The first kid in line started toward the cone shuffling at a painfully slow pace, small step after small step, all the way down and all the way back. The second kid did the same, so did the third and so on. When it came to my turn, I also shuffled all the way down and all the way back, just like they had all done.

The class continued to shuffle along at a painfully slow pace and when it was finally over, the teacher blew the whistle and I skated off and around the rink toward my parents. The teacher, taking note of this, promptly told both me and my parents that I no longer needed the class.

Here's the Point.

Why did I shuffle all the way down, and all the way back when I had the ability to ice skate? What would make a six year old do such a thing?

I believe it's fear. From a young age, I (as well as many of us) have a fear of standing out and being different. Fear guides us to shuffle along when we have the ability to skate.

How many times do we shuffle in life because everyone else around us is shuffling? How many times do we let the fear of being different outweigh our God-given ambitions, talents and abilities? Daily, we make decisions to shuffle along with the crowd, when (maybe for years) we've had the ability to get up and skate away.

Culture sells us a lie that we can't achieve great things. It tells us that greatness is too far out of our reach. At the root of this lie is fear, and we frequently buy into it through many seemingly unconscious decisions to shuffle rather than to stand out.

Don't you want more out of life than just shuffling? I believe you do. What will you do today to stop shuffling and skate away from the crowd? It may be difficult, but it will be worth it. Stop believing the lie that you will never discover your purpose and become something great.

Skate away from fear. Skate away from the anxiety of looking weird. Skate away into what you know you're able to do, because you've been assigned a great purpose. There is a wonderful plan for your life.   Your life can be full of deep meaning if you'll step out onto the ice. It may be slippery, but you've been given the tools to get moving—now go out and skate.

Reflection and Discussion Questions

1. What fears are you believing about yourself today?
2. What will you do today to stop shuffling with the crowd and skate on your own?

Watch the accompanying video "Shuffling" at https://www.youtube.com/watch?v=KfJ2vPBsim4

Notes

7

"Picking Up a Hitchhiker"

What's the story?

The word 'why' contains a nuclear-like power. Why, can be a question as well as an answer. It can be a reason or an excuse. It can be the beginning of a pursuit as well as the end of a dream. It's the justifier for a laser-like focus in life as well as a reason to call off the search. Why—feel it as you say it.

As a statement, the word 'why' can make you bold, driven and focused. As a question, it can make you tighten down the screws, broaden the horizon, and dig a little deeper. It can be a cry, a scream or a silent whisper in a dark night of the soul.

Deep down, everything we do is rooted in the word, why. For fun, try to think of something you do that isn't linked to why

—it's impossible. Everything has a why, although, not all why's can be known.

Every once in a while, I find myself more on the question end of the word why.

My wife, Jen, and I were visiting Virginia Beach one summer to officiate a wedding; there's a why. Following the wedding, we sought to enjoy a little of what the beach had to offer; yet another why. (You get the point)

On our way to the beach, we found ourselves stuck front-and-center in six lanes of traffic; three off to the right, and two more off to the left. As we waited for the light to change, I noticed a couple near the road dressed from head to toe in traditional Indian garb. They stood out to us, and apparently we stood out to them as well because they began walking in the midst of the three lanes of traffic in between us to approach our car. As surely as the sun was shining on the beach that day, they then knocked on our window and asked us for a ride.

Let me pause this story for a second to beg the question why? Why did they pick our car in the sea of beachgoers? Why did they ask us for a ride? Why were they at the exact intersection we were at looking to go, in the direction we were going? How did they know about my affinity for picking up hitchhikers; even those wearing full leather gear with a spiked collar and a human-sized leather duffel bag? (I'll save that tale for another story and a point)

I looked at Jen for her response. She already knew my response because of our marriage tenure. At her affirmative and adventurous shrug, we said, "Come on in." The pair jumped into our car and at green, we were on our way.

Now, what do you do in moments like this, with two hitchhikers dressed in Indian garb sitting in your back seat? Well, for us, we started our search for, why, by asking a series of questions to our guests.

"Where are you from?" I asked. "Baltimore," they replied. Ok, I wasn't expecting that one. "Where are you going?" I asked next. "To our hotel just up the road," they indicated as they pointed me in the right direction. After a little driving and a lot of internal sifting of this information, we arrived at their hotel. Right before they got out, I asked a final question. "Can you tell me what your names are?" The gentleman replied, "My name is Andy and this is my wife Jenny."

After introducing ourselves as the other Andy and Jenny in the car, we sat in awe, staring at each other for more than a few awkward moments. After Andy and Jenny, from Baltimore, left our car, this Andy and Jenny, from Edinboro, sat for an additional ten minutes thinking, "What just happened?"

Here's the Point.

To this day, we have not figured out the, why, of that day on the road to Virginia Beach. And strangely enough, I believe the point wrapped in that thought—some whys are unanswerable. Sometimes, we just don't know why. Often things happen in life that we just don't understand. What do we do in response to those whys?

Maybe a good place to start is to recall your whys. You are created for a purpose. You are living a story that is significant. What you do really matters and because of that, it is essential to get out of bed, to put your feet to the floor, and set out to do what's been put before you to do; whether it's raising kids, going to work, creating a system, writing a book, leading a team, or encouraging a neighbor.

You don't have to have all the answers to move forward when crazy things happen, and you know as well as I do, that crazy things do happen.

Are you going to move forward when you don't know why? Are you going to do what you have to do, and keep pushing, even when what you're striving for hasn't materialized yet?

My hope is that you let the, why, you are certain of push you forward past the seemingly unanswerable whys in life. And in doing so, I hope you can find freedom to move forward fearlessly and pursue relentlessly the, why, you were created for, equipped for and designed with precision to fulfill.

Reflection and Discussion Questions

1. What "why's" in your life have you been unable to answer? How do you respond?

2. Take some time to recall your "whys". What is your purpose—your "why"?

3. Will you choose to move forward when you don't the why? Will you take the steps you need to keep moving, even when you can't see what's up ahead?

Watch the accompanying video "Picking up a hitchhiker" at https://www.youtube.com/watch?v=tk5AoAVTYkc

Notes

_____
_____
_____
_____
_____
_____
_____
_____
_____
_____
_____
_____
_____
_____
_____
_____
_____
_____
_____
_____
_____
_____
_____

8

"Spiders and Forgiveness"

What's the Story?

I spotted a jurassic-spider in my garage one morning as I was preparing to get in my car and leave for the day. It was the most gargantuan 8-legged predator I had even seen. I'm sure that one prick from its fangs could have made me Spiderman. As much as I would have enjoyed the superpowers of casting webs and walking up walls, what I really desired that day was the superpower of being able to unsee something horrifying. The truth is; however, there are some things that just cannot be unseen.

I spotted the jurassic-spider, it spotted me, and I now had to do something about it. My first thought was to step on it, but that would have left an enormous mess. My second thought was to grab a jar and catch it. I went for the second option and sought out a jar large enough to contain it. Without losing any time, I grabbed a jar and held it up to the monster and it jumped—right into the jar. I put the lid on tight, poked a few holes on top so it could breathe and began inspecting my capture. Did it need to eat? What would I feed it? Something big? A rat? I had no idea what I had just captured, but now I had to do something with it.

First, I had to figure out what type of spider I was dealing with. I scoured google images of spiders and still couldn't identify it on my own. I needed the help of an expert and the only place I could think of bringing jurassic-spider was to the zoo.

I loaded up my jar, and drove to the local zoo. The gate attendant let me in and asked how she could help me. I told her that I had a spider and that I needed help identifying it. She was obviously intrigued as she let me and the spider in to see the zookeeper. Upon inspection, it was identified as a wolf spider. (It seemed obvious to me that its dad was a wolf, and its mom was a spider.) The zookeeper kept it and later released it back into its habitat—which made me sad because I couldn't come back and visit it. I hoped; however, it didn't want to come back and visit me.

Here's the Point.

I found a wolf spider, and I didn't want it in my house. This was an issue. Sometimes there are things that creep their way into our lives that need to be taken care of, or removed. When we spot these things, we're left with some choices. Will we turn a blind eye and hope for the superpower to unsee them, or will we make the choice to remove the things that become a hindrance in our lives?

What we need to do when these things creep into our lives is to remove them, and remove them quickly. If we let them linger they may invite their friends.

Think back to the spider imagery with me, one spider is bad, but a whole house full of spiders is terrifying. They make horror films out of things like this. No one wants their life to become a horror film.

Let's translate this spider example into something more practical. Let's call it unforgiveness. If we let unforgiveness alone in our life, it can multiply, grow, and become horrifying. It can destroy relationships, tear families apart and work against all that's good in life. It has been said that harboring unforgiveness is like drinking poison and waiting for the other person to die.

We need to work to keep the semi-small things small and forgive others. In order to move on, maybe today you need to

forgive. Today, make the choice to let the past go, and work
toward moving forward.

    We'd do well to kill the spider of unforgiveness—or maybe
take it to the zoo where it belongs.

Reflection and Discussion Questions

1. What have you allowed to creep into your life that should have been removed?
2. If there someone in your life you need to forgive?

Watch the accompanying video "Spiders and forgiveness" at https://www.youtube.com/watch?v=oUkb3pUwB4c

Notes

9

"Yellow Zone and Taking Risks"

What's the Story?

Living in the yellow zone is another term for living in life's sweet spot. Many years ago, I spent my summers developing students in a camp setting as a camp counselor. This is where I first began using the term, yellow zone. If you've ever spent time as a camp counselor, you know the fun of dangling from ropes, climbing tall things, sending students into caves, eating crappy food and drinking spoiled milk—it's great. Plus, there's a meager salary that accompanies this adventure, which makes it all the better. Whenever a new group of students would come to camp, we'd teach and encourage them to live in the yellow zone.

Let me explain.

Think of a stop light. There are red lights, green lights and yellow lights. Each color is symbolic of a subsequent action. Obviously, green means go, yellow means caution and red means stop. Now, imagine these actions juxtaposed with your life as zones to live in. First, we have the green zone where life is comfortable, predictable and not at all challenging. Second, we have the yellow zone where an appropriate amount of stress or challenge begs that we take appropriate risks and proceed with caution. Then we have the red zone where we are paralyzed with fear and cannot move. We're forced in the red zone to literally stop—a very scary place to be. Have you ever been there? To this day, I can clearly remember one time when I was in the red zone.

As a boy, my dad and I fished a lot. On one such fishing trip, as a seventh grader, my dad invited me to fish with him in rural Pennsylvania's Allegheny Forest. We were on a mission to catch brook trout and we were successful that day, catching lots of them. After catching and releasing about forty fish, I was covered in fish guts and smelled like a brook trout.

I remember meandering down the stream, away from my dad, in search of more fish when I looked up and noticed a large bear who also seemed to notice me. He began paralleling my movement just across the water from me, following me down the stream. This wasn't good. I smelled like what he wanted to eat. As I thought about being eaten by a bear in the Allegheny Forest, my knees began to lock up, my muscles began to stiffen and I grew paralyzed with fear. I was living in the red zone for sure.

The only thing that came to mind was to take out my bug spray and cover myself in it. You have to love the strategic thoughts of a seventh grader. If he was going to eat me, I would not give him the satisfaction of tasting good. I pulled out my bug spray and began pump spraying it all over my body. As I did so, I squeaked out the word "dad" as best as I could in hopes that my dad would hear me and come to my rescue. Fortunately, he heard my whimper and as he came to my rescue, the bear was startled and fled. I was so grateful that my dad got me out of the red zone. He wanted to stay and fish some more, but I saw my salvation as a green light to go home for the day.

Here's the Point.

You can't live life paralyzed with fear in the red zone. You also can't live life in the green zone where things are easy, comfortable, predictable and routine. Just as I encouraged my campers many years ago, now I want to encourage you too to live in the yellow zone. If you want to live in life's sweet spot, growing and thriving; challenged and challenging those around you; resilient and adaptable to a changing world surrounding you; you need to live in the yellow zone.

How do you live in the yellow zone? You can start by taking risks. Risk taking works to pull us out of our comfort zone and challenges us to rise to the occasion. It breaks us out of life's routines. Risk taking builds inside of us the grit to keep us going in difficult circumstances. Risk reminds us that the fabric of greatness is woven inside of us. You were made for more than you know. What risks are you going to take this week?

In a survey taken of people age 95 and older, one question was asked of them: What would you do differently in life? The greatest common response was overwhelmingly, "I'd take more risks."

Let me ask you again—what risk are you going to take this week so you can live in the sweet spot, or yellow zone in life?

Reflection and Discussion Questions

1. How do you live your life? With fear, in the red zone; predictable, in the green zone; or challenged in the yellow zone?

2. What risks are you taking, to push yourself from the red or green zone, into the yellow zone?

3. What risks will you take this week so you can starting living in the sweet spot in life?

Watch the accompanying video "Yellow zone and taking risks" at https://www.youtube.com/watch?v=C_vjrZch-4U

Notes

10

"Vacationing"

What's the Story?

Everything we needed for an extended stay away from home was packed up and placed under the tonneau cover of my Ford truck. Jen was in the passenger seat and I was behind the wheel. It was time for our annual vacation. As the key turned to put power to the pistons, I said to Jen, "So where do you want to go this year on vacation?" Now, in some marriages the timing of this question would spark fear and outrage, but for Jen and I, this is how we adventure together. Without missing a beat, Jen replied, "How about Yellowstone?" I echoed back, "Sweet, let's go!" And we were off.

We drove all night long taking one brief pause along the side of the road for a quick nap. Did you know it is illegal to stop on the side of a road for a nap? Let me tell you just as the police officer told me, "Son, this is illegal, get going." We took his not-so-subtle hint, and got going until we finally rested our eyes on the land of Tatonka and Old Faithful and the majestic Yellowstone National Park.

After exploring most of the day amongst hundreds of other fellow adventurers, we began locating a potential campsite to rest at for the night. We found our first campground and went in to inquire about vacancies. They were full. We ventured onto the next one, and the next one, and the next one—each time met with the same response, "We're full." Maybe we'd find better luck at a hotel. We traveled to a few hotels and then some motels. No vacancy. By this time, we were starting to wonder if we'd ever find a place to stay for the evening. We went back to Yellowstone and asked the park officials if there was anywhere else in the park, around the park, or even remotely close to the park in which we could stay.

The officials pointed us in the direction of a small private campground 14 miles away with 132 camp sites. This seemed very promising. Hopefully, this was going to be the place where we could camp for the evening. Their directions led us down a two lane highway which turned into a one lane dirt road and then into an overgrown path. Finally we reached our destination. There, we saw RV's of all types, cars, trucks, and even a VW bug parked in camp spots and yet, no place for the Ford. They were full too. We turned around and headed back towards the park. On the way back, we saw a hotel in the distance that we hadn't been to yet. Seizing the opportunity I went in, practically begging for a room in the inn. I was hoping for a miracle, or a stable—anything! They were full too.

Mustering all the ingenuity I had, I returned to Jen and said, "We're going to sleep in the back of this truck tonight, right here in this parking lot." And that's just what we did. We unsnapped the tonneau cover, rolled it back just enough for the two of us to crawl in, and then snapped it shut with 4 inches of clearance above our noses. We slept from 3 a.m. that night until 8 a.m. the next morning.

When I woke up, I popped my hand up out of the tonneau cover, reached for the latch and dropped open the tailgate prior to crab crawling out of the rear of the truck bed. At that moment I realized how popular it was to watch the sunrise over the Wyoming skyline from one's hotel balcony. Seemingly, everyone who stayed in the hotel that night ventured onto their porch to watch me crawl out of my truck.

Here's the Point.

Just as I wanted a particular place to stay that night, I should have planned for it.   Great adventures often require great planning. Great results come from well-calculated steps. If you want a particular outcome in life, due diligence requires careful planning.

We leave far to many aspects of our lives to chance; hoping to hit the lottery with the dreams, goals and vision for our lives. Do you want a great business, a great family or a powerful legacy? If so, develop a plan with intentional, systematic steps to reach your goal.

Can you imagine the distance you'd be able to travel in pursuit of your vision with just one small step taken each day? Desired ends are the result of intentional means. Seize the opportunity, make the plan, take the step—today.

Reflection and Discussion Questions

1. What are you leaving to chance that you should be intentionally planning for?

2. What steps will you take today to seize the opportunities in front of you?

Watch the accompanying video "Vacationing" at https://www.youtube.com/watch?v=fNH2awtS0tc&t=55s

Notes

11

"Moral of the Pectoral"

What's the Story?

As a Physical Education major in college, I learned how muscles function, how to keep physically fit and how to teach others to keep physically fit as well. However, I didn't learn what I call the moral of the pectoral until I became a life coach.

It was upper body workout day and I was at the gym ready to go. After warming up my muscles, I went to the Smith machine, which is a barbell fixed within steel rails to allow only vertical movement. I put a good amount of weights onto the barbell and began my workout. As I slowly started to pull the bar down, I felt something begin to pop in my pectoral which was followed by an amount of pain that I can't even begin to describe. The pain was so bad that I almost passed out. I slowly put the bar onto the rack and waited until the pain subsided enough to sneak out underneath the machine.

As the pain subsided, I wondered if my injury wasn't as bad as I first thought. I waited a few days prior to seeking medical attention hoping this to be true. It wasn't until I looked at myself in the mirror and noticed one pectoral sitting lower than its neighbor, that I decided to ask a physical therapist friend for some next steps. Without hesitation, my friend indicated that I was to go to the doctor immediately. My injury appeared to be a torn pectoralis major. I made an appointment to see a specialist soon thereafter.

Have you ever seen a doctor do a slight head tilt upon looking at something on your body? It's a pretty good indicator that there may be some severity to your injury. As my doctor did the head tilt, he instructed me to get an MRI of the injury as soon as possible; and at 7AM the next day, I was heading toward the imaging center for my pectoral scan.

Details haven't always been my strength and I may or may not have been paying attention as to where the imaging center was. It appears I wasn't paying attention. I discovered that I was alone in a room with no secretary, fish tank, giant imaging machine and no insurance forms to fill out. (It was the last of these that fully convinced me I was in the wrong spot.) I did, however; see a delivery person walking by whom I questioned as to the location of the imaging center. He directed me up five floors to an office with a secretary, fish tank, imaging machine and lots of insurance forms to fill out—this looked about right.

I gave the secretary my name and sat down in the waiting area. While there, I was received with some strange looks from patients next to me. I didn't think much of it, but continued minding my own business. After a few minutes, a nurse nervously approached me asking if she could be of assistance. I explained to her that I was Andy Kerr and needed an image done of my pectoral. She explained to me that I was in the breast exam center. "Ok" I said, "let's get it done then." "No, sir, this is the female breast exam center," she said. That was a game-changer. She pointed me next door and I promptly exited with a little less pride than I brought into the room.

Next door, I finally got an MRI. It was confirmed that I had torn my pectoralis major. Soon after, I had surgery to repair what was torn.

Following the surgery, the doctor and I had an evaluation together with some good news and bad news. The good news was, the surgery was a success. I would recover to have full range of motion with a total repair of the muscle. The bad news was, I waited longer than I should have to get the repair done. There was a significant amount of scar tissue which made the repair difficult and scarring inevitable. There went my opportunity to be a shirtless model.

Here's the Point.

My torn pectoralis major was an extremely serious injury, yet I didn't act upon it quickly. I waited until the pain subsided, which made me question its severity and subsequently fail to act quickly to fix it. The doctor confirmed the commonality of this as he said, "People often wait to fix injuries, which creates more scar tissue, more difficult repairs and less likelihood of a full recovery."

This is the moral of the pectoral: don't wait to fix your problems, because repairs become more difficult with time. The longer we wait to get help, the greater the potential for physical, emotional and relational scar tissue to build up.

Is there a relationship in need of mending? Is there an issue that needs addressed? Is there an addiction that needs named and corrected? Is there something physically wrong or a health problem in need of healing? If so, take a small step in the direction of healthiness and success today.

Reflection and Discussion Questions

1. What problems are waiting to fix?
2. What is keeping you from taking the steps towards mending the physical, emotional and relational scar tissue?
3. What small step toward healing can you take today?

Watch the accompanying video "moral of the pectoral" at https://www.youtube.com/watch?v=MbazQhBHXgE

Notes

_____

_____

_____

_____

_____

_____

_____

_____

_____

_____

_____

_____

_____

_____

_____

_____

_____

_____

_____

_____

_____

_____

_____

12

"Horses"

What's the Story?

What are you afraid of? For most people the question, "What are you afraid of?" generates an answer with google-like speed. Maybe it's crowds; maybe it's heights; maybe it's public speaking; maybe it's finding goo on your suit as you're public speaking on a high platform—everyone is afraid of something.

For me, it's horses. I'm afraid of horses. There, I said it. Horses scare the hooves off of me. I'll tell you why in just a second, but first, let's think about the precursor to fear. Discovering the why behind your fear is the first step away from fear. Let me say that again, only differently. Fear is like a knot that keeps us bound and unable to extend ourselves to our full potential. Knowing why you are afraid of something is the first step to untangling the knot that fear is in life.

Horses were part of my upbringing. My family boarded them and we grew up with horses around our house constantly. One day, when my mom went riding, she got thrown from her horse. She lay undiscovered in a ditch with a separated shoulder until hours later when I found her. After discovering her, I sprinted at top speed to call an ambulance and get her help. Imagine being nine years old and finding your mother hurt by a giant horse—that evil beast. She recovered, but the knot of fear was set in me that day. My parents did not give up on horses and we continued to have them around our house. I had given up on them though. I was not comfortable around them any longer.

That same year, one of my closest buddies lived across from our pasture. To get to his house, I had to cross our horse pen encircled by an electric fence. I would wait until the horses weren't looking, and when it appeared safe to cross, I would sprint toward my buddy's house. One day, as I was returning to my house, I ducked under the fence to begin my wait and sprint ritual. At first, all went according to plan. Mid-sprint; however, I noticed that one of our horses took notice of me and started chasing me. I didn't take my eyes off of the beast as I continued my sprint towards home and I completely misjudged where the electric fence ended. I proceeded to hit it at full speed with my face taking the brunt of the impact—zap. After twenty-five stitches and many crimsoned cleaning towels, I was really done with horses.

I did not have to face this fear until later on in life when Jen and I were on our honeymoon. We had the opportunity to go horseback riding along the coast of the ocean. How romantic this should have been. For those around me, it was. But for me, I was scared out of my mind. Not wanting to let the beauty of this moment escape (and more so not wanting to freak out in front of my new bride) I faced my fear, got on the horse and on my honeymoon began working to untie the fear that had bound me many years prior.

Here's the Point.

Fear ties us up inside. Fear needs untied and untangled. The first step to untangling fear is to understand how and why our fears are there. Once we understand the how and why of our fear, the unloosening and unraveling can take place.

The experiences I had with horses as a nine-year-old tied me up. It never went away. I didn't always see it or feel the fear, but it was there. It wasn't until my honeymoon that this fear surfaced again. Fear doesn't go away. It lies beneath the surface until it is untangled, unraveled and eliminated. Once I thought back to that event, and started to chip away at what was making me afraid, I could start to move forward.

Is there a fear you have neglected to fix? Is there a knot binding you that needs untangling and unraveling? Maybe you got the google-speed answer when I asked you, "What are you afraid of?" earlier. Have you ever stopped to think of the why behind this answer? Maybe this is the key to you untethering a fear that keeps you bound. Who do you need to talk to today to face that fear? What decision can you make today to begin untying fear?

We cannot live and thrive when we're in knots. Living fully is living freely. We can run toward our full potential when we're untethered to fear, and you can begin a journey free from fear today.

Reflection and Discussion Questions

1. What are you afraid of? Why?
2. Who can you talk to today about facing that fear?
3. What decision(s) will you make today to start untying that fear?

Watch the accompanying video "Horses" at <u>https://</u>
<u>www.youtube.com/watch?v=Smr9gJP9oU8</u>

Notes